The Cup on the Counter and Other Poems

Alberta Hargreaves

BookLeaf Publishing

India | USA | UK

The Cup on the Counter and Other Poems ©
2024 Alberta Hargreaves

All rights reserved.

No part of this publication may be
reproduced, stored in a retrieval system, or
transmitted, in any form or by any means,
electronic, mechanical, photocopying,
recording or otherwise, without the prior
written permission of the presenters.

Alberta Hargreaves asserts the moral right
to be identified as author of this work.

Presentation by *BookLeaf Publishing*

Web: www.bookleafpub.com

E-mail: info@bookleafpub.com

ISBN:9789358315790

First edition 2024

DEDICATION

For my mum, who showed me how to be strong.

The Cup on the Counter

Kitchen, 6am, quiet,
Steps across the cold tile floor,
A mother begins breakfast,
Already dressed.
The birds outside are singing
Their morning song,
Frost is still on the window.
She makes some toast,
The toddler will rise first,
Then some eggs,
The child will be next.
She prepares the coffee,
For brewing,
But doesn't.
The cup in front of her,
Resting on the counter.
It explodes, shatters,
Blinded, both eyes pierced,
Screaming, bleeding,
Gurgling on the blood,
Heating the tiled floor,
the rage.
Silence.
She leaves the cup,
The coffee is ready to brew,

Because the father will be last.

Skirt Section

Basket by my leg, I look
At the skirt section in
front of me. I pick up,
A pink mini skirt, the tag
reads 'slut', the black mini skirt,
Tag says 'slag'.
I pick up a midi-skirt,
Tag reads 'classy but frigid'.
A maxi skirt, 'just frigid.'
Thigh length, 'perfectly acceptable'
But it rides up my thighs,
Hips too wide, for dainty fast fashion.

Forgetting

An old man gets dementia,
But his family is the one that's sad,
He doesn't remember their names.
They're the strangers.

A woman is in a car crash,
She hits her head on the window,
She wakes up surrounded by,
Faces she doesn't know.
They're strangers.

A group of friends fall apart,
They meet up decades later,
They all start to talk,
But there's no conversation.
They're strangers to each other.

An adopted child reaches out,
To their true parents,
They look the same but,
When they meet they are different.
They're related strangers.

A famous man walks down a street,
No one recognises him,

No one remembers, his great thing,
But he realises,
They're all strangers.

Masking

When I see my reflection,
I ask myself; Who am I?
I can be anyone, blend in anywhere,
But only enough to survive.
They know I am not like them,
They know I am wearing something,
They have never had to wear,
Uncanny valley, not quite like them,
But close enough.
When I unmask, I feel at ease,
But also a longing sadness;
How long did I hide this?
How long before I can stop?
How do I know when I unmask?
If you've been masking for so long,
When does the mask just become your face?
A long process they say,
A hard process they say,
I wish I could switch it off with a button,
I can sometimes,
But when I do, I am a husk,
I am a collection of hobbies, references, ideas
I don't feel any identity,
I don't feel a part of one organism,
A multitude of ideas clashing together,

To create what I believe is myself,
But I don't know.

7

Stacking Cat Food Near the Tills

Stacking cat food near the tills,
Pick them up, put them down,
Answer questions, serve the customers,
It's 8am, not busy, being in since 5.
A man, comes in, sees me,
Corners me, I have to stop stacking,
Cat food, I'm near the tills,
I know I am on camera,
I should be calm, my coworkers are close,
But fight or flight kicks in,
I can't run, I am working, my body is,
screaming at me, but I don't move,
He continues talking, I am panicking,
So much I can't breath, I can't understand,
What he's saying. He gives me a penny,
Says something about it bringing him,
Luck. He winks and walks away,
I breath. My coworker asks if I'm okay,
I say yes, of course, I am a woman,
I'm used to it. Then, I go back to
Stacking cat food.

Falling Into A Book

I flick through the pages,
The smell of dust and age,
I find my bookmark, take it out,
I fold the spine, I read
The first word.

The ink is dripping from the page,
They're morphing out of sync,
My breath is hitched,
Anticipation,
The black surrounds,
Consumes me,
When I begin to fall.

I see words in front of me,
As air flows by,
A light begins to shine below,
I don't know how long I fell for,
An eternity or a second,
But I fall,

Into another place,
Where I am the creator,
Imagination flows out,
I am the spectator,

Lost inside a universe,
Different from my own.

Internal Winter

I am cold, constantly,
Internal winter, my fingers,
Growing dark from the inside,
Frost bite creeping outwards.
Tears, frozen in the pipes,
My mind swirling around,
The thoughts blizzarding,
Blinding yet each one,
Still stings, whipping across,
My skin.

A Girl Named Rose

A young girl, tame and timid, her name rose,
She never dressed up, wearing the same clothes,
Riding her horse, numb from head to toes,
Never one to brag, never the one that shows,

Sweet as a petal, but dark was her prose,
what happened that year, nobody knows,
Yet what can be said is that he lost a nose,
And she buried his body, she had to dispose

It was said by her family, that they disclose,
That she wasn't the killer, no one apposed
No one knew he was in the meadows,
She smirked at where she chose,

It was the place he was meant to propose,
She knew what he hid in the shadows,
And it would follow wherever he goes,
So it was up to her, left him to compose,

But now she's sure they'll oppose,
The plan will fall like dominoes,
Their verdict will surely transpose,
Only then they'll truly predispose,

The morning after, she was exposed,
Next thing she knew, she was inclosed,
In a stake and flames, above were crows,
Once she was dead, the ground froze,

But from that place, from fate I suppose,
That's where petals fall from a black rose.

Food Waste

Don't be a child and eat your veg,
Or it's own world at your knife's edge,
Lack of awareness to a problem so plain,
When all you need to do,
Stop putting food down the drain.
Check the sell-by dates,
And look where to store,
To put the right things in the right drawer.
Yet these tiny things add to causation,
Which turns into a global situation.
Food Waste in Uk, Canada, Mexico, China,
America,
Equal to the entire net of Sub-Saharan Africa.
Losses at harvest, processing can't be their fault,
It's the consumers and retail which are the
assault,
1.6 billion tonnes in the bin per year,
And somehow the problem still isn't clear.

Ew.

15

Ew. She wears jeans,
Whilst I'm wearing my pretty,
Pink skirt. She wears,
Trainers, or sweatshirts,
Band t-shirts! She even eats,
Everything that she wants,
Chicken nuggets, burgers,
I just eat the low carb salad,
But even that is too much.
Does she even go out? Or,
Does she stay at home,
Playing video games, and
Watching movies.
Ew.
I am just like the other,
Girls, why can't she be?

Being Scared as an Adult

Being scared as an adult,
Is much more difficult,
Then being scared as a child.
Hiding, under the warmth of,
My bed duvet, and cradling,
A teddy bear does not stop,
The war waging in my head,
I cannot hide from the things,
That scare me. Even, if I reach,
A place where I am free, where,
All is tranquill, a calm ocean,
Where I can sit as one, it is only,
A fleeting moment.

Ivy

I am forced out of this muddy trench,
The light leagues above me.
I have a job to do.
I grow. Towards the light,
But the canopy lays on top of me,
The enemy lines.
A rainstorm is coming,
The bombardment against me.

So I'll climb.
Slow at first,
Crawling low to the ground.
I am scared,
I cling to the tree,
No man's land,
My leaves are left behind me,
My troops deployed.

The rain begins to fall,
Beating down my front lines,
The salvo from the heavens.
The icy wind picks up,
I need to get there quick,
Or I will freeze with it.
I break out into a sprint,

But now I am exposed.

I'm almost there,
My allies are gone,
There's nothing left but me.
Stretching, so far.
I feel the canopy,
The branches like bayonets,
The leaves like barbed wire,
I push and squirm.
So close, I can feel the fresh,
Then heat hits my skin.
I won.

Alcohol

Just a sip. A tiny amount,
Hardly a trace in my system,
Then it's suddenly silent.
50% or 4%, doesn't matter,
Something about it, a switch,
Is flipped, and I am normal.

A night out, city centre,
The lights are blurred, I forgot,
My glasses at home. An arm,
Wrapped around mine, in a huge,
Group, we are walking to the club,
Loud, lots of people, something,
I usually avoid, but this alcohol,
In my system makes me love it.
I walk arm in arm with these people,
They don't know me sober, not really,
But they in this moment, accept me,
When the morning comes they won't,
But right now, we are walking arm in arm,
I am part of a group.

Waking up the next day, the feeling doesn't,
Ware off immediately, I hope to find,
The people gave sent me a message, pictures,

Of the fun night from before, but there is,
None. Throughout, the day the creeping feeling,
That I am alien to everything around me.
I am the lone wolf, weakened by its
Isolation.

I don't hear anything for days,
But when I see them again, through,
A chance meeting or some other means,
They act as if we are best friends,
Confused, I act like that to, mirroring,
Them, blending in. But then, they offer,
Me a shot. I do it, why not?
Suddenly, I realise they were my friends,
This whole time, it was me, who didn't
Reach out. That's all. The alcohol,
Tells me to relax and I do.

Turning 20

When I turn 20, some will say,
It's my first steps into my adult,
Life. I should be grabbing life,
By the throat and making my,
Way through it, with determination.
That's what they say.
But I am quite happy to float,
I have dreams, goals,
But I am still happy to float.
Many people say I should,
Flow into the current of the river,
Which goes down from its,
Mountain origins, and into a,
Pulsing river. But I want, to float,
On the surface, I will reach where,
I want to go, soon enough,
But I want to dream a little longer.
Turning 20, makes the tug of the,
Current even stronger, I want to,
Float above the water for,
Just a little longer.

Fidget Cube

Click. Click. Click.
Playing with the fidget,
Cube in my Pocket.
Tap. Tap. Tap.
Alone, I walk down,
The Street,
Click. Click. Click.
There is a man,
Approaching,
Tap. Tap. Tap.
My breath, lost,
Panic swelling.
Click. Click. Click.
I try to cross,
But there are cars,
Racing by.
Tap. Tap. Tap.
No breathing, hands
Sweating, I can't,
See.
Click.
Bright lights. Gushing wind.
Tap.
He isn't far off now.
Click.

He looked at me.
Tap.
Eye contact.
Click.
A step away.
Tap.
He walks past,
The air around me brushes,
I can breathe again.

Storm

A storm is coming.
The cows are huddled,
The seagulls in pairs,
But I'm all alone,
Feeling the cold coming,
Slowly.

I'm unprepared.
My mind is racing,
Nerves crashing against my head,
The blood thundering,
Flashes of pain.

I need to leave.
Quickly, hurriedly, swiftly,
But I don't know where to go,
Anywhere but a storm.

Down on my knees,
Hands together,
Wishings for sanctuary,
Away from here,
Mercy for my soul.

Nesting

I surround myself,
With my found treasures,
Like a magpie, I gather,
Anything which catches,
My eye. I nest in the corner,
Of the living room,
Bean bag, food,
I-Pad. Surrounded by,
Fairy Lights.
Warmth, comfort,
Tucked into a blanket,
Watching stupid videos,
I'll forget by tomorrow.

Her Fault

Walking down the short snicket,
She saw him approach,
He didn't say a word to her,
Just grabbed her by the throat.

She was on the floor,
Panites in her mouth,
Looking at the stars,
Hoping he'd come out.

Every movement burnt,
His breath, heavy smoke,
She didn't even know him,
Just some random bloke,

He left her there,
Limp and lifeless,
"Her fault, her fault,
Silence means yes."

The walls screamed it's your fault,
Don't speak a word,
"Her fault, her fault,"
That was all that she heard.

She took a shower,
Hoping to be clean,
"Her fault, her fault"
Is all that she could see.

She went to work after,
Standing at the till,
"Her fault, her fault,
She did it for the thrill,"

Crying, she took her break,
Stood in the bathroom stall,
"Her fault, her fault"
Was written across the wall.

Running home,
She felt like she was bare,
"Her fault, her fault."
Was written everywhere.

Bath water, lukewarm.
The act she would commit,
"Her fault, her fault."
She sighed and made two slits.

Blackening vision, fading lights,
Her final act of will
"Her fault, her fault,
At least she wasn't killed."

Runaway Dead Girl

Runaway dead girl,
History of drug use girl,
Regular runaway girl,
Drifter scoundrel girl,
Her fault girl,
Skirt too short girl,
Wrong place, wrong time girl.
No news coverage girl,
No investigation girl,
Only families looking girl,
Too old to care girl,
20 year old girl,
30 year old girl,
Dead girl,
Raped girl,
Victim of a murder girl.

Like A Puppet

Severe the ties that hold her heart
Destroy her hope and dreams
Don't let her run,
Don't let her hide,
Pull the strings
Control her like a puppet.

Open the door for her to walk
But don't let her get too far
Don't let her see
Don't let her hear
Pulls the strings
Control her like a puppet

You are in charge, she must obey
Punishments will be in order
Don't let her stand
Don't let her breath
Pull the strings
Control her like a puppet

Never let her out of sight
She may do something bad
Don't let her go
Don't let her be

Pull the strings
Control her like a Puppet

She has escaped, the ties are loose
She has undone the knot
You must catch
You must chase
Grab the strings
Chain her like a puppet.

Tuesday Morning at Sandsend

The sea climbs high,
As I watch,
Apple in my mouth.
I want to read but,
I can't take my eyes off the sea.

It's calling out to my soul,
The sand between my toes chuckles,
Because it knows.
The dogs bark, the waves sing,
All in perfect harmony,
A symphony which can only be understood,
By minds which are in the present.

The winds cold,
Yet the coffee cup in my hand,
And the fire inside warms me.
Hair flying around, I never
Move to correct it, just letting it,
Be free.

Looking out to the horizon,
On this stormy day,
I feel small,

But it's a comfort,
I know my place in this world.
So I just sit,
Soft indie playing in my ears,
And I hope I can feel this again.